Science in Infographics

HABITATS

Jon Richards
and Ed Simkins

Gareth Stevens
PUBLISHING

Please visit our website, www.garethstevens.com.
For a free color catalog of all our high-quality books,
call toll free 1-800-542-2595 or fax 1-877-542-2596.

Cataloging-in-Publication Data

Names: Richards, Jon. | Simkins, Ed.
Title: Habitats / Jon Richards and Ed Simkins.
Description: New York : Gareth Stevens Publishing, 2020. | Series: Science in
infographics | Includes glossary and index.
Identifiers: ISBN 9781538242957 (pbk.) | ISBN 9781538242971 (library bound) |
ISBN 9781538242964 (6 pack)
Subjects: LCSH: Habitat (Ecology)--Juvenile literature. | Information visualization-
-Juvenile literature.
Classification: LCC QH541.14 R47 2020 | DDC 577--dc23

Published in 2020 by
Gareth Stevens Publishing
111 East 14th Street, Suite 349
New York, NY 10003

Printed in the United States of America

CPSIA compliance information: Batch #CS19GS: For further information contact Gareth Stevens,
New York, New York at 1-800-542-2595.

CONTENTS

WHAT IS A HABITAT?

A habitat is an area where a plant or an animal lives and the conditions found there. The type of habitat depends on a wide range of variables, including the climate, the surrounding features, the position on the planet, and the type of rock found there.

Coniferous forests – filled with evergreen coniferous trees, these regions have cold winters and mild summers.

134°F
HIGHEST RECORDED TEMPERATURE
FEBRUARY 10, 1913,
FURNACE CREEK,
DEATH VALLEY,
CALIFORNIA, USA

Types of habitat

Ocean – the largest habitat, covering more than 70 percent of the planet, it is dominated by salty water and ranges from rich coral reefs to the dark ocean abyss.

Mountains – high altitude habitats that vary the farther up you travel, from lush rainforests to open grassland to bare rock.

Mediterranean – found in regions with hot, dry summers, these regions contain scrub vegetation.

Tropical rain forests – these regions are warm and wet all year round and contain high concentrations and variations of plants and animals.

Temperate grasslands – large areas of grassland found in temperate regions, they support large herds of grazing animals.

Tundra – cold, treeless regions where the ground just below the surface remains frozen all year round. This frozen layer is called permafrost.

Deserts – dry regions of the world that receive very little precipitation throughout the year.

-90°F
LOWEST RECORDED TEMPERATURE
(FOR A PERMANENTLY INHABITED PLACE) 1933, **OYMYAKON, RUSSIA**

Temperate forest – containing a mix of evergreen and deciduous trees, these regions have four distinct seasons every year.

MEGHALAYA IN INDIA RECEIVES

467 INCHES
OF RAIN EVERY YEAR – MORE THAN ANYWHERE ELSE.

IN CONTRAST, SOME SCIENTISTS BELIEVE THAT THE **DRY VALLEYS IN ANTARCTICA** HAVE NOT SEEN RAIN FOR NEARLY

2 MILLION YEARS.

Tropical grassland – areas of large grassland with long dry seasons and short rainy seasons.

Poles – cold regions around the planet's two poles, these areas are covered by thick sheets of ice all year.

TEMPERATE AND EVERGREEN FORESTS

Forests found in cooler regions of the world have short growing periods during the spring and summer months. At other times, plants and animals have to cope with cold, sometimes freezing, temperatures.

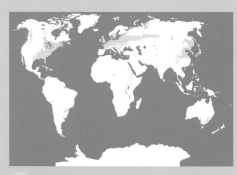

Temperate forest

Temperate forests

These habitats are found in regions of the world lying between the tropics and the polar areas. They have four distinct seasons: spring, summer, autumn, and winter. In spring, deciduous trees sprout buds that grow into leaves by summer. These then turn brown and fall off during autumn and the tree stands dormant during winter.

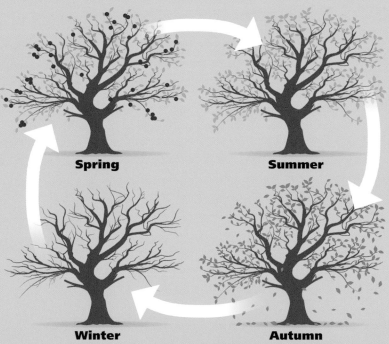

Spring

Summer

Winter

Autumn

Some forests have such a thick canopy (the layer of branches and leaves) that little light reaches the forest floor in summer. This means that few plants grow there.

Plants living in temperate forests include broad-leafed trees, such as oak and beech, as well as ground-flowering plants including bluebells.

Taiga

The northern coniferous forest is also known as the taiga. It is the largest land habitat in the world and covers about 17 percent of Earth's land surface, mostly in a huge belt that runs across the northern hemisphere.

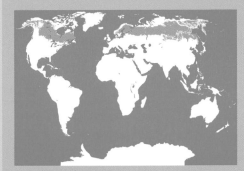

Coniferous forests or taiga

17%

Oak

Beech

Bluebells

Hedgehog

Fox

Plants include conifers and pines, as well as grasses and sedges.

Grasses **Fir Tree** **Pine Tree**

Animals living in the taiga have to survive long, cold winters and short summers. Some do this by hibernating or entering a long, sleep-like state. These include bears. Others travel (migrate) away during the winter and return in the summer. These include geese.

Goose **Bear**

Some animals, such as hedgehogs, hibernate through the cold winter months. Other forest animals include foxes and deer.

Temperature and rainfall

Temperate

Average temperatures are about **50°F** (10°C), with warm summers averaging about **68°F** (20°C).

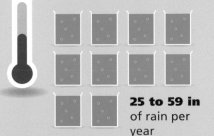

25 to 59 in of rain per year

Taiga

Average temperatures range from about **14°F** (-10°C) to **32°F** (0°C) in winter and about **59°F** (15°C) to **68°F** (20°C) in summer.

12 to 20 in of rain per year

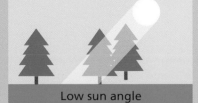

Low sun angle

The sun is low in the sky (at an angle of 63.5–47°) because of the northerly latitude, so less solar energy reaches the ground. Snow cover also reflects a lot of solar energy.

RAIN FORESTS

These are some of the richest habitats on the planet, supporting an enormous range of plants and animals. While most of them are found in warm tropical regions close to the equator, a handful lie in cooler temperate regions.

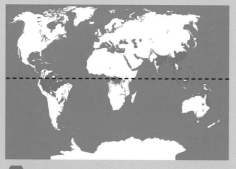

◆ **Rainforests**

Tropical rain forests

This habitat covers just 6 percent of Earth, but contains more than half its plant and animal species.

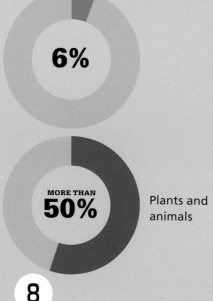

·········· Tropical rain forests

6%

MORE THAN 50%

Plants and animals

Layers of the rain forest

Emergent – the tallest trees, called emergents, poke above the canopy.

Canopy – the branches and leaves of the trees form a thick layer called the canopy, which lets little light through.

Under canopy – below the canopy, young trees wait for older trees to die so they can take their place, while lianas grow up from the forest floor, using trees for support.

Shrub level and forest floor – very little light reaches the forest floor, restricting the amount of plants that can grow here.

Rain forest plants include exotic flowers, such as pitcher plants and orchids, and huge trees.

Orchid

Pitcher plant

Boa constrictor

Jaguar

Animals include big cats, such as tigers and jaguars, apes, birds of paradise, and large snakes, such as boa constrictors.

Temperature and rainfall

Rainforests get more than **100 inches** of rain every year.

= 6 in

The temperature varies little and stays between **77–86°F** (25-30°C) all year round.

TEMPERATE RAIN FORESTS

These are found in cooler regions, including North America, East Asia, Australia, and New Zealand. They have a long wet season, but also a dry season.

Deer

Plants include tall redwoods, Douglas fir, ferns, and mosses. Animals include black bears, deer, and cougars.

Douglas fir

305 ft

Statue of Liberty

Redwoods are some of the largest single living things on the planet, and can grow to heights of more than **330 feet** (100 m).

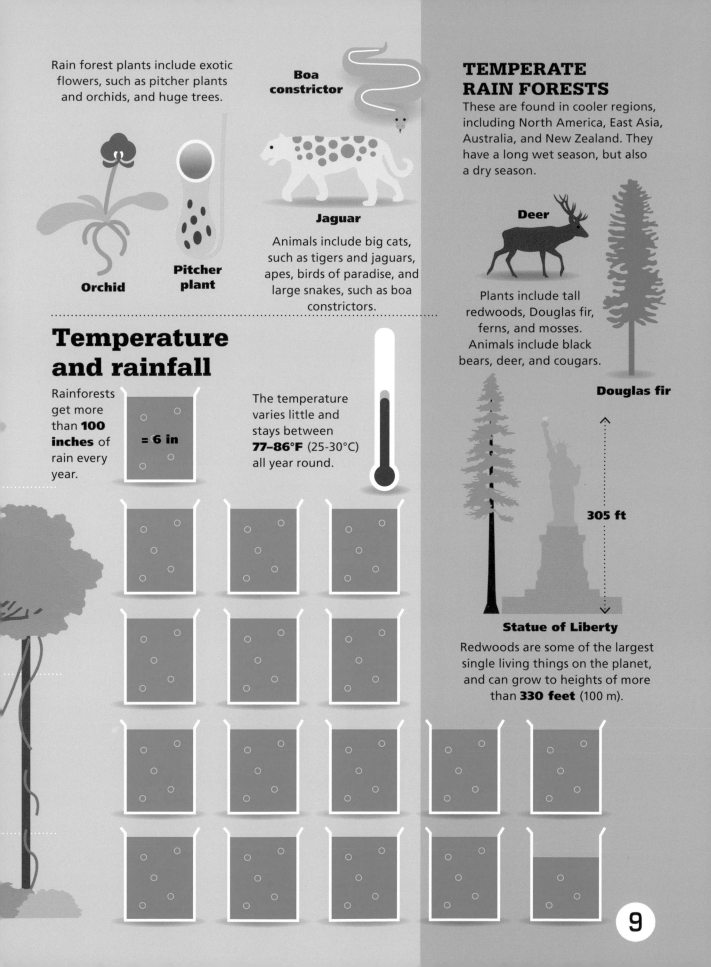

DESERTS

Deserts are regions that receive less than 10 inches (25 cm) of rain in an entire year. Although many of them are found in hot regions close to the equator, there are also some that lie in cooler temperate regions, where local features and conditions prevent a lot of rainfall.

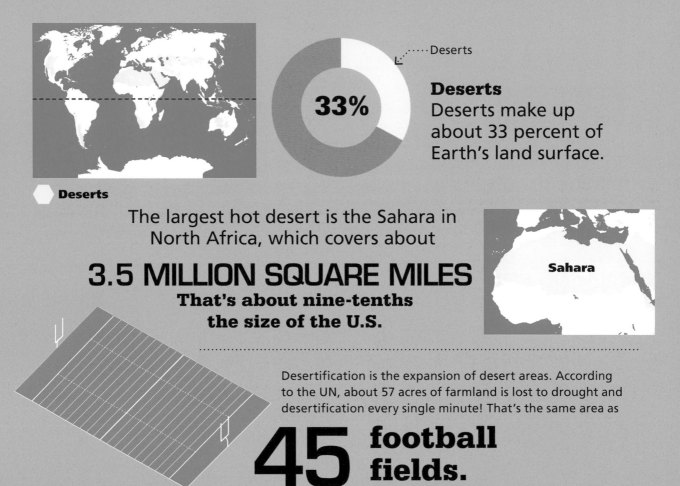

Deserts

33%

····· Deserts

Deserts
Deserts make up about 33 percent of Earth's land surface.

The largest hot desert is the Sahara in North Africa, which covers about

3.5 MILLION SQUARE MILES
That's about nine-tenths the size of the U.S.

Sahara

Desertification is the expansion of desert areas. According to the UN, about 57 acres of farmland is lost to drought and desertification every single minute! That's the same area as

45 football fields.

Temperature and rainfall

Hot deserts have an average annual temperature of **68–77°F** (20-25°C), but can get higher than **120°F** (50°C). Temperatures at night can fall below **32°F** (0°C).

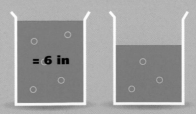

= 6 in

Deserts get less than **10 inches** of rain every year.

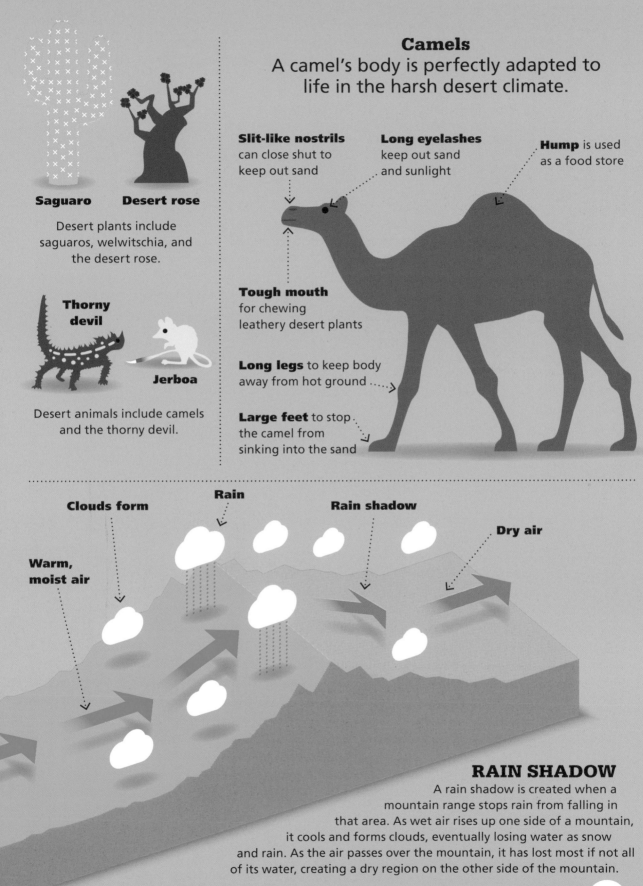

Saguaro **Desert rose**

Desert plants include saguaros, welwitschia, and the desert rose.

Thorny devil

Jerboa

Desert animals include camels and the thorny devil.

Camels
A camel's body is perfectly adapted to life in the harsh desert climate.

Slit-like nostrils can close shut to keep out sand

Long eyelashes keep out sand and sunlight

Hump is used as a food store

Tough mouth for chewing leathery desert plants

Long legs to keep body away from hot ground

Large feet to stop the camel from sinking into the sand

Clouds form

Rain

Rain shadow

Dry air

Warm, moist air

RAIN SHADOW
A rain shadow is created when a mountain range stops rain from falling in that area. As wet air rises up one side of a mountain, it cools and forms clouds, eventually losing water as snow and rain. As the air passes over the mountain, it has lost most if not all of its water, creating a dry region on the other side of the mountain.

MOUNTAINS

Because they cover a wide range of altitudes, mountains support a variety of habitats. These vary as the conditions change the higher up the mountain you travel.

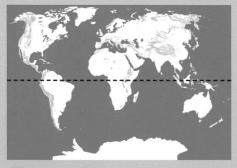

Mountains

Air temperatures drop by 0.9-1.1°F (0.5–0.6°C) every 328 feet (100 m) you climb up a mountain.

41°F   **3,280 ft**

45.5°F   **1,640 ft**

50°F   **0 ft**

Mountain zones

Nival zone – only mosses and lichens grow here

Alpine zone – made up of meadows

Subalpine zone – made up of coniferous forest

Tree line

The uppermost limit where trees grow is known as the tree line. Above this point, conditions are too harsh for trees.

Montane zone – made of a mixture of deciduous and coniferous forest

Foothills zone – made up of deciduous forest

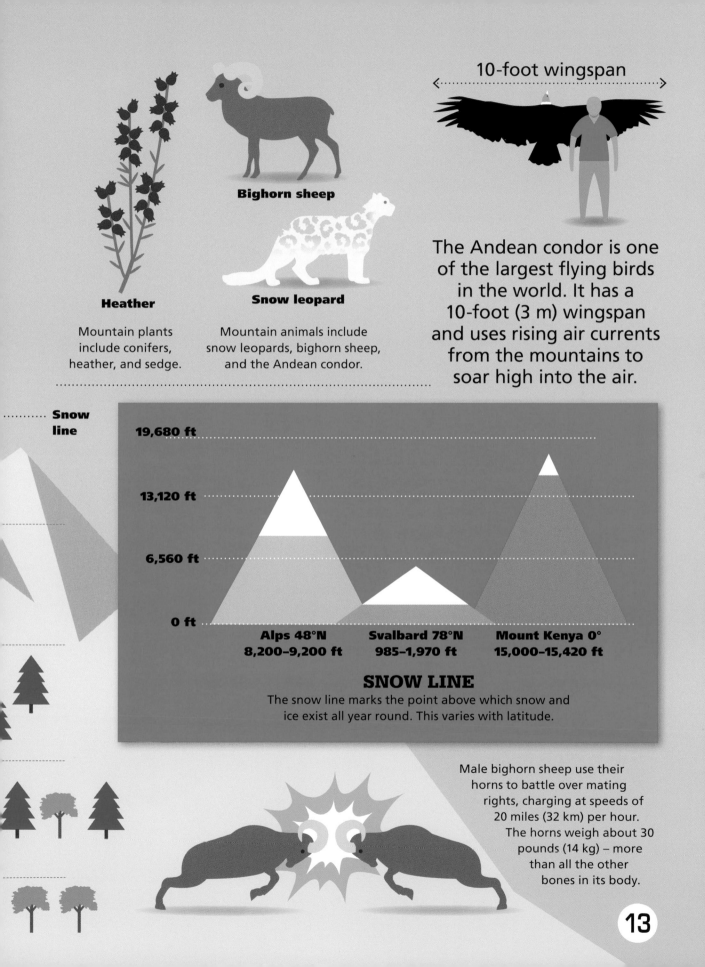

10-foot wingspan

Bighorn sheep

Snow leopard

Heather

Mountain plants include conifers, heather, and sedge.

Mountain animals include snow leopards, bighorn sheep, and the Andean condor.

The Andean condor is one of the largest flying birds in the world. It has a 10-foot (3 m) wingspan and uses rising air currents from the mountains to soar high into the air.

Snow line

19,680 ft	
13,120 ft	
6,560 ft	
0 ft	

Alps 48°N
8,200–9,200 ft

Svalbard 78°N
985–1,970 ft

Mount Kenya 0°
15,000–15,420 ft

SNOW LINE

The snow line marks the point above which snow and ice exist all year round. This varies with latitude.

Male bighorn sheep use their horns to battle over mating rights, charging at speeds of 20 miles (32 km) per hour. The horns weigh about 30 pounds (14 kg) – more than all the other bones in its body.

13

GRASSLANDS

Huge grasslands are found on every continent, except Antarctica. They support enormous herds of grazing animals.

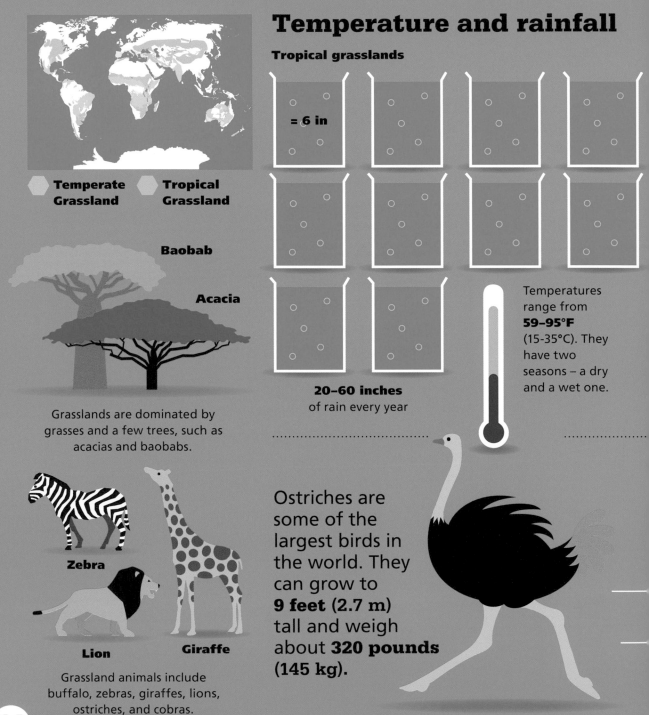

Temperate Grassland

Tropical Grassland

Temperature and rainfall

Tropical grasslands

= 6 in

20–60 inches of rain every year

Temperatures range from **59–95°F** (15-35°C). They have two seasons – a dry and a wet one.

Baobab

Acacia

Grasslands are dominated by grasses and a few trees, such as acacias and baobabs.

Zebra

Lion

Giraffe

Grassland animals include buffalo, zebras, giraffes, lions, ostriches, and cobras.

Ostriches are some of the largest birds in the world. They can grow to **9 feet (2.7 m)** tall and weigh about **320 pounds (145 kg)**.

The dry periods of tropical grasslands force many of the animals living there to move long distances in search of water and food. These migrations can involve millions of animals traveling hundreds of miles.

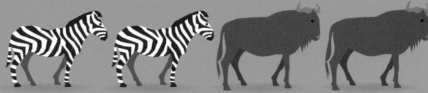

The Great East African migration involves more than **1.5 million wildebeest, 200,000 zebras,** and **thousands of antelopes.**

Temperate grasslands

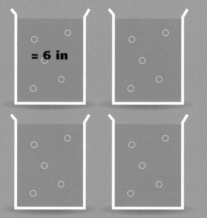

= 6 in

12–24 inches of rain a year

Four seasons. Temperatures range from **14°F** (-10°C) in January in northern grasslands to **82°F** (28°C) in July.

During every migration, about 250,000 wildebeest and 30,000 zebras are killed by predators, thirst, hunger, and exhaustion.

250,000   30,000

Many plants in tropical grasslands are xerophytic. This means that they have adapted to life in dry conditions. For example, acacias have small, waxy leaves to reduce water loss.

Acacia leaves

Prairie dog

Ostriches can run at speeds of up to **43 miles per hour** (70 kph). Each stride covers **16 feet** (5 m).

Prairie dogs are small mammals that live in the grasslands of North America. They dig burrows and live in communities called towns. Usually, these cover about 0.5 square mile, but the largest ever discovered covered an area of

25,000 sq miles

– that's bigger than the state of West Virginia. It was home to about

400,000,000

prairie dogs.

TUNDRA

Beyond the large coniferous forests and close to the polar regions is the tundra. This is a habitat where conditions are so harsh that no trees grow and where any growing season lasts a few short weeks.

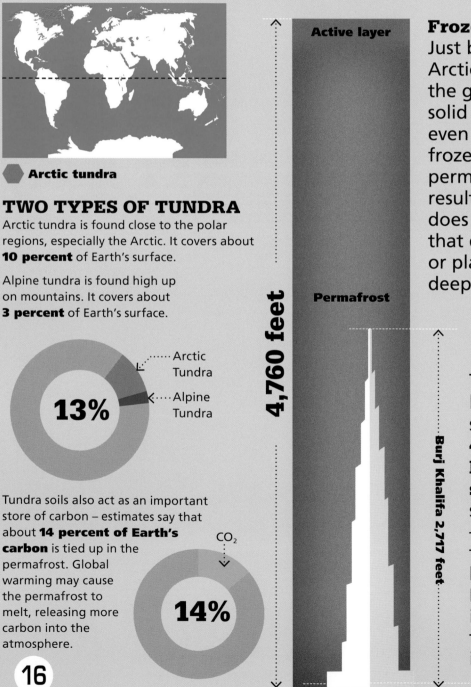

● **Arctic tundra**

TWO TYPES OF TUNDRA

Arctic tundra is found close to the polar regions, especially the Arctic. It covers about **10 percent** of Earth's surface.

Alpine tundra is found high up on mountains. It covers about **3 percent** of Earth's surface.

13%

····· Arctic Tundra

←···· Alpine Tundra

Tundra soils also act as an important store of carbon – estimates say that about **14 percent of Earth's carbon** is tied up in the permafrost. Global warming may cause the permafrost to melt, releasing more carbon into the atmosphere.

CO_2

14%

Active layer

Permafrost

4,760 feet

Burj Khalifa 2,717 feet

Frozen subsoil
Just beneath the Arctic tundra surface, the ground is frozen solid all year round, even in summer. This frozen layer is called permafrost. As a result, the tundra does not have animals that dig deep burrows or plants that have deep roots.

This frozen layer may stretch down **4,760 feet below the surface** in some regions – that's nearly twice the height of the Burj Khalifa in Dubai, the tallest building in the world.

Tundra is found above 60°N latitude in North America and 70°N latitude in Eurasia – the difference is caused by the warmer summers experienced on the larger landmass of Eurasia.

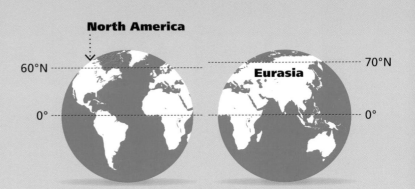

North America
60°N — 0°
Eurasia
70°N — 0°

Temperature and rainfall

Arctic tundra

= 6 in

Arctic tundra regions have about **15 inches** of rain a year, but can get nearly **80 inches** of snow in a year.

Temperatures range from about **39°F** (4°C) in summer to **-25°F** (-32°C) in winter.

Alpine tundra

= 6 in

Alpine tundra regions have between **3** and **25 inches** of rain a year.

Temperatures can reach about **54°F** (12°C) in summer and in winter go down to about **0°F** (-18°C).

The word **tundra** comes from the Finnish word **"tuntria"** which means **"treeless land."**

Arctic poppy

Sedge

Snow goose

Wolverine

Reindeer

Tundra plants include grasses, sedges, and mosses, as well as the Arctic poppy.

Tundra animals include wolverines, reindeer, musk oxen, snow geese, and Arctic skuas.

THE POLES

The extreme northern and southern parts of the world are some of the most inhospitable on the planet, with freezing days and long periods of complete darkness when the sun fails to rise above the horizon.

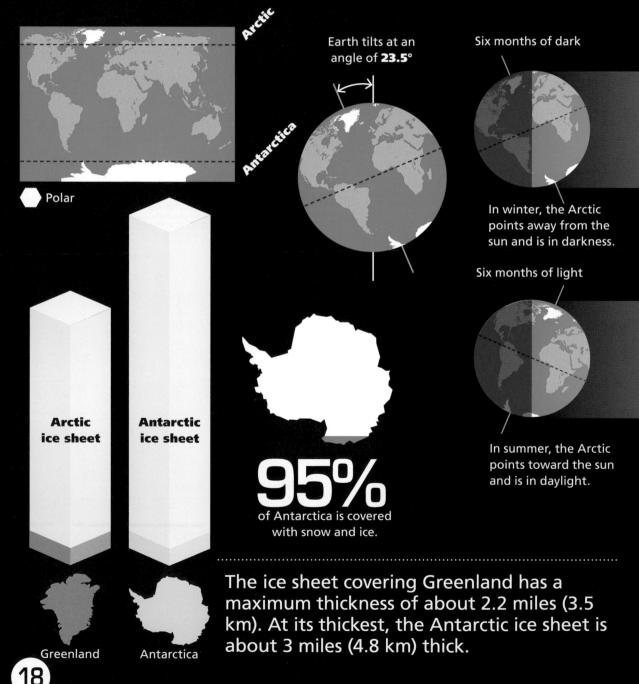

Arctic

Antarctica

Polar

Earth tilts at an angle of **23.5°**

Six months of dark

In winter, the Arctic points away from the sun and is in darkness.

Six months of light

In summer, the Arctic points toward the sun and is in daylight.

Arctic ice sheet

Antarctic ice sheet

95%
of Antarctica is covered with snow and ice.

Greenland

Antarctica

The ice sheet covering Greenland has a maximum thickness of about 2.2 miles (3.5 km). At its thickest, the Antarctic ice sheet is about 3 miles (4.8 km) thick.

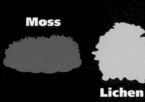

Moss

Lichen

The only plants found in these regions are small grasses, lichens, and algae that can survive the harsh conditions.

Polar bear

Emperor penguin

Polar animals include polar bears, arctic foxes, crabeater seals, emperor penguins, and fulmars.

Polar bears are good swimmers. One was recorded swimming for **nine days straight, covering 427 miles (687 km).** That's about the distance from Washington, D.C., to Boston!

Arctic sea ice levels have been decreasing. In November 2016, Arctic sea ice extent was about 3.51 million square miles (9.08 million sq km), the lowest November figure ever recorded. It was about 750,000 square miles (1.95 million sq km) lower than the average November figures for 1981–2010.

1981–2010
Average

4.26 million sq miles

2016

3.51 million sq miles

Krill

Hippopotamus

Every year, huge amounts of tiny plankton flourish in Antarctic waters, attracting some of the biggest creatures on the planet. In a single day, an adult blue whale will eat about 40 million tiny krill, weighing in at more than **7,700 pounds** (3,500 kg) of food – that's about the same weight as a hippopotamus!

The lowest ever temperature was recorded at Vostok Station in Antarctica. It was

-128.6°F.

Since 1960, average winter temperatures on the Antarctic Peninsula have increased by 10.8°F (6°C).

COASTS

Coasts are where the sea meets the land. This creates a habitat that changes regularly as the seas rise and fall with the tides and where features are carved out by the power of the ocean.

The world has about

385,000 MILES

of coastline

– almost long enough to stretch **to the moon and back**.

Nearly 2.4 billion people, about one-third of the world's population, live within 60 miles (100 km) of the coast.

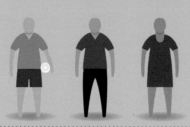

Current sea level

50 FT

– the greatest tidal range, found at the Bay of Fundy, Canada, equivalent to a three-story house.

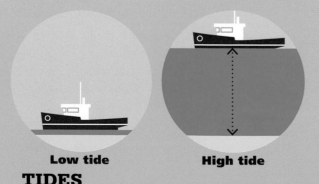

Low tide   **High tide**

TIDES

The daily rise and fall of sea levels is caused by the gravitational pull of the moon and sun on the water.

Sea level last ice age period

During the last ice age period, sea levels were more than 390 feet (120 m) lower than today – almost the height of **the Great Pyramid at Giza**.

Waves can hit with a pressure of

7,000 LB
per square inch.
This force can create a wide range of diverse features. These include:

Cliffs – formed by erosion and collapse of the shore

Arches – erosion of part of a cliff, creating a hole or arch

Stack – when an arch collapses, leaving a stack

Flamingo

Crab

Sea lion

Jellyfish

Grasses

Coastal plants include salt tolerant grasses and sedges.

Sedge

Coastal animals include wading birds, sea birds, seals, sea lions, crabs, and jellyfish.

Coral reefs
Coral reefs are formed from the rocky skeletons of tiny creatures, called polyps. Some of the reefs today started forming about 50 million years ago.

Coral Polyp

Polyps are translucent (see-through) – they get their colors from brightly colored algae called zooxanthellae.

Great Barrier Reef

The world's largest coral reef is the **Great Barrier Reef** off the coast of Australia. It stretches for more than 1,600 miles (2,600 km) and is about half the size of Texas.

1%

25%

Coral reefs cover less than 1 percent of the ocean floor, but they support about 25 percent of all marine creatures.

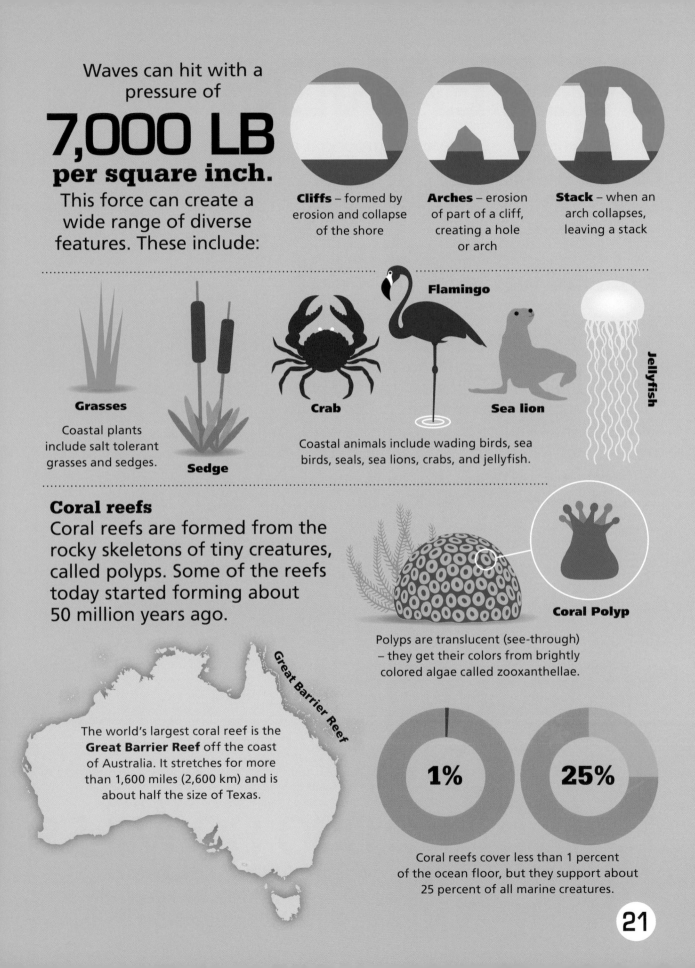

WETLANDS

Wetlands are regions where the ground is waterlogged for at least part of the year. These habitats are found close to the sea, where saltwater floods the ground, or further inland in freshwater bogs, marshes, and swamps.

Types of wetland

Mangroves

These wetlands are named after the trees that grow in them. They have long stilt roots that stand out of the mud and keep the plant above the water. They also have special respiratory roots, called pneumatophores, which stick above the mud and water and have small openings to let air in.

Stilt roots

Pneumatophores

BANGLADESH

INDIA

The Sundarbans in India and Bangladesh is one of the largest saltwater swamps on the planet, covering about

3,860 SQ MILES
– THAT'S ABOUT THE SAME SIZE AS THE ISLAND OF HAWAII.

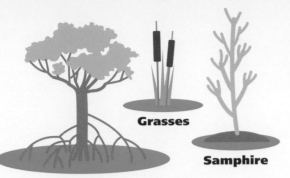

Wetland plants include mangroves, grasses, and samphire.

Wetland animals include catfish, wading birds, shrimp, dragonflies, and alligators.

Tidal marshes

These are found on river systems that are close enough to the coast to have their waters rise and fall every day with the ocean tides.

Freshwater marshes

These form in areas where water collects and cannot drain away easily. They range in size from small potholes to huge regions, such as the Florida Everglades, which cover about 730 square miles (1,900 sq km).

Riparian wetlands

These are formed when a river overflows and floods the surrounding area. Every year, the waters of the Amazon flood up to 96,500 square miles (250,000 sq km), an area the size of the state of Michigan.

Peatlands

Peatlands form when material from dead plants and animals decomposes slowly and starts to build up. This forms a layer of peat, which contains a high level of organic matter.

RIVERS AND LAKES

Rain falling on high ground and spring water that bubbles up from underground flow downhill and collect into channels to form streams. These join together to create rivers, which flow into lakes or the sea.

Profile of a river

Source

Upper course – v-shaped valley with narrow valley floor and a steep riverbed

Middle course – wide valley with small meanders and a floodplain

Lower course – very wide valley with large meanders. River carries a large amount of sediment.

Mouth

During the dry season, the area covered by the Amazon is about 42,500 square miles.

42,500 sq miles

135,000 sq miles

In the wet season, this increases to about 135,000 square miles.

The Amazon is the widest river in the world. At times it can be 25 miles (40 km) across, which is wider than the English Channel.

24

RUSSIA

Lake Baikal

Lake Baikal in Russia is the largest lake in the world.

Its maximum depth is

5,315 FT,

DEEP ENOUGH TO SWALLOW THE EMPIRE STATE BUILDING **MORE THAN 3.5 TIMES.**

It holds about 5,500 cubic miles of water **– about one-fifth of the world's freshwater.**

< ⋯⋯⋯ **World's freshwater**

< ⋯⋯⋯ **Lake Baikal**

There are about

117 MILLION
LAKES ON EARTH

and about **90 million of these (about 77 percent)** cover less than 2.5 acres – less area than two football fields.

When combined, the shorelines of the world's lakes measure **250 times** the distance around the equator.

Duck

Crocodile

River dolphin

Freshwater animals include otters, river dolphins, water birds such as ducks and geese, freshwater fish such as sturgeon, crocodiles, and frogs.

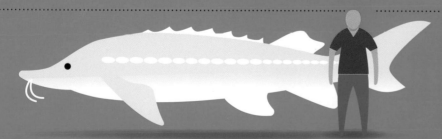

Sturgeon are the largest freshwater fish in the world. The biggest ever recorded was about **20 feet (6 m) long.**

Water lilies
Freshwater plants include water lilies.

25

OCEANS

Seas and oceans cover more than 70 percent of our planet. They offer a broad range of habitats, from the deep ocean to shallow seas.

Pressure

...... Surface

...... 3,280 ft

CRUSHING PRESSURES

The average depth of the ocean is 12,400 feet (3,800 m). The deepest part is Challenger Deep, which is 36,000 feet (10,994 m) below sea level. Pressures here are 1,000 times greater than at sea level.

...... **Average depth**
12,400 ft

x500

...... 16,400 ft

x1,000

...... 32,800 ft

...... **Challenger Deep**
36,000 ft

SWIRLING CURRENTS

Huge ocean currents carry cold and warm water around the globe, spreading heat and maintaining different habitats on land and sea.

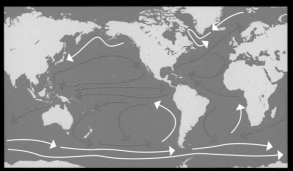

—— Warm water   —— Cold water

Pacific Ocean

←←←

Normal year

Pacific Ocean

→→→

Warm water   **El Niño**
Cold water   **year**

EL NIÑO

El Niño is a change in the pattern of warm and cold water in the Pacific Ocean. This can produce large changes in conditions, causing droughts in some parts of the world and torrential storms and flooding in others. This change can happen every three to five years.

Hydrothermal vents

These are areas where superhot water gushes out from the seafloor. The hot water is rich in nutrients and minerals and attracts some unique wildlife.

Ocean giants

Seas and oceans are home to some
of the biggest animals on the planet:

Lion's mane jellyfish – about 115 feet long

Blue whale – about 100 feet long

Giant squid – about 40 feet long

Whale shark – about 43 feet long

Oarfish – about 26 feet long

Ocean sunfish – about 8 feet long

Japanese spider crab
– about 12 feet across

Giant clam – about
4 feet across

750°F
– the temperature of
water gushing out of
a hydrothermal vent.

Giant tube worms
live on hydrothermal
vents and can be
6.5 to 10 feet long.

Giant kelp – up to 100 feet

Giraffe – up to 20 feet

Towering plants
Giant kelp is a giant
seaweed, which is
a type of algae. It
attaches to the ocean
floor in cool, clear
waters and stretches
up for 100 feet
(30 m). It grows in
thick forests that are
home to thousands
of animal species,
such as sea otters.

ARTIFICIAL HABITATS

They may look like harsh habitats where few wild plants and animals could survive, but many living things have adapted to thrive in urban environments, living close to thousands of people. And towns and cities are one of the few habitats that are increasing in size.

Growing habitat

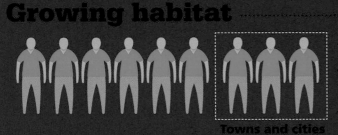

Towns and cities

In 1950, about one-third of the world's population lived in towns and cities.

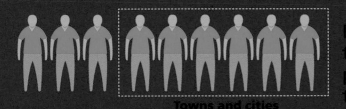

Towns and cities

By 2030, a projected two-thirds of the world's population will be living in towns and cities.

IN 1950, THERE WERE JUST TWO MEGACITIES, WITH POPULATIONS OF MORE THAN 10 MILLION.

TODAY, THERE ARE 21 MEGACITIES.

RICH HABITATS

Even a small back garden will have a rich variety of wildlife. A study of a garden in the United Kingdom found:

More than 1,000 plant species

80 species of lichen

4,000 species of invertebrates

WILDLIFE CORRIDORS

To promote wildlife conservation, corridors of grasslands and woodlands can be built from one wildlife habitat to another so that animals can move freely.

285

– the number of bird species that have been spotted in New York's Central Park.

PERFECT PERCH

Skyscrapers offer an ideal spot for falcons and other birds of prey to nest. They also give the birds a good view of the surrounding area in their hunt for food.

There are an estimated

4,000,000

rats living in Paris

– almost twice the human population (2.2 million).

ARTIFICIAL REEFS

These are man-made structures that are deliberately sunk so that marine plants and animals can grow on them. One of the biggest was the aircraft carrier USS *Oriskany*, which was more than 885 feet (270 m) long, sunk on May 17, 2006.

GLOSSARY

algae
Simple plants that usually live in water. They include seaweeds.

altitude
The height of something in relation to sea level or ground level.

baobab
A short tree with a very thick trunk and large edible fruit, common in grassland regions.

canopy
The highest branches of trees in a forest.

carbon
A chemical found in coal, for example, that can be harmful to the atmosphere. Trees and permafrost absorb carbon.

climate
The weather of an area over a long period.

coniferous
Something that is made up of or related to conifer trees, such as a coniferous forest.

deciduous
A type of plant, such as a tree, shrub, or bush, that loses its leaves in autumn every year.

desertification
The process in which fertile land becomes desert as a result of drought, deforestation, or poor farming methods.

drought
A long period without rain, leading to water shortages and crop failures.

evergreen
A type of plant that keeps its leaves all year.

grasslands
Large open regions covered in grass and often used for grazing.

habitat
The natural home of an animal or plant.

hibernation
When an animal or plant spends the winter in a dormant or sleep-like state.

ice age
A long period of low temperatures on Earth's surface, causing the expansion of polar ice sheets and glaciers.

liana
A long, woody vine that grows from the ground and climbs up trees to reach the forest canopy.

megacity
A very large city with a population of more than 10 million. Mumbai in India and Shanghai in China are examples of megacities.

migration
The movement of animals between places.

permafrost
A layer of soil beneath the surface of the ground, which remains frozen all year.

plankton
Microscopic organisms that drift in water.

pneumatophores
Specialized roots that poke above water and help plants to breathe in waterlogged soil.

precipitation
Rain, snow, sleet, or hail that fall to the ground.

respiration
The process that uses oxygen and sugars to produce energy, water, and carbon dioxide.

samphire
A plant similar to parsley that grows on rocks and cliffs near the sea.

sea ice
Frozen seawater that floats on the water's surface. Sea ice covers about 12 percent of the world's oceans.

sedge
A grass-like plant that grows in wet ground in temperate and cold regions.

stilt roots
Supporting roots that prevent shallow-rooted trees from falling over and hold the plant above any floodwater.

taiga
The swampy regions of coniferous forest found in northern latitudes.

temperate
Refers to the parts of the world that lie between the tropics and the poles.

tidal range
The measurement difference between high tide and low tide.

tropical
Refers to parts of the world that lie on either side of the equator.

tundra
A vast, flat, treeless Arctic region of Europe, Asia, and North America in which the subsoil is permanently frozen.

xerophyte
A plant that has adapted to live in an area with very little water, such as a desert.

Websites

MORE INFO:
www.dkfindout.com/us/animals-and-nature/habitats-and-ecosystems/
This page is packed full of amazing facts and information about habitats and ecosystems.

kids.nationalgeographic.com/explore/nature/habitats/
This website has information about many different plant and animal habitats.

MORE GRAPHICS:
elearninginfographics.com/category/k12-infographics/elementary-school-infographics/
This web page has tons of school-related infographics.

www.kidsdiscover.com/infographics
This website contains a whole host of infographic material on many different subjects.

Publisher's note to educators and parents: Our editors have carefully reviewed these websites to ensure that they are suitable for students. Many websites change frequently, however, and we cannot guarantee that a site's future contents will continue to meet our high standards of quality and educational value. Be advised that students should be closely supervised whenever they access the Internet.

INDEX